MINE
MINE
MINE

Uhuru Portia Phalafala

University of Nebraska Press / Lincoln

The poems on pages 62 and 72 were previously published
as "History in My Body" in *Years of Fire and Ash*, edited by
Wamuwi Mbao (Johannesburg: Ad Donker, 2021).

The University of Nebraska Press is part of a land-grant institution
with campuses and programs on the past, present, and future
homelands of the Pawnee, Ponca, Otoe-Missouria, Omaha, Dakota,
Lakota, Kaw, Cheyenne, and Arapaho Peoples, as well as those
of the relocated Ho-Chunk, Sac and Fox, and Iowa Peoples.

∞

The African Poetry Book Series is operated by the African Poetry
Book Fund. The APBF was established in 2012 with initial support
from philanthropists Laura and Robert F. X. Sillerman. The founding
director of the African Poetry Book Fund is Kwame Dawes, Holmes
University Professor and Glenna Luschei Editor of *Prairie Schooner*.

Library of Congress Cataloging-in-Publication Data
Names: Phalafala, Uhuru Portia, author.
Title: Mine mine mine / Uhuru Portia Phalafala.
Other titles: African poetry book series.
Description: Lincoln : University of Nebraska Press, 2023. | Series:
African poetry book series | Includes bibliographical references.
Identifiers: LCCN 2022045795
ISBN 9781496235152 (paperback)
ISBN 9781496235664 (epub)
ISBN 9781496235671 (pdf)
Subjects: LCSH: Gold mines and mining—South Africa—
Johannesburg—Poetry. | Miners—Diseases—South
Africa—Johannesburg—Poetry. | Miners—Wounds and
injuries—South Africa—Johannesburg—Poetry. | BISAC:
POETRY / African | LCGFT: Poetry.
Classification: LCC PR9369.4.P47 M56 2023
DDC 821.92—dc23/eng/20220927
LC record available at https://lccn.loc.gov/2022045795

Set in Garamond Premier by N. Putens.

The living owe it
to those who
no longer can speak
to tell their story
for them
—CZESŁAW MIŁOSZ

We are not strangers
to the end of peace
We have known women widowed
without any corpses of husbands
because the road to the mines
like the road to any war
is long and littered with casualties
even those who still walk and talk
—KEORAPETSE KGOSITSILE

MINE MINE MINE

In 2018 a historic silicosis class action lawsuit against the mining industry in South Africa was settled in favor of the miners.*

---

*The miners are dead.
  1. Bringing legality into matters of state vs. property reproduces colonial violence.
  2. How about land?
  3. What about white capital?
  4. What about Black overlords?
  5. Some are still buried under mine shafts!
  6. An unpayable debt: No favor.
  7. An incalculable catastrophe explored in six movements.

PART 1

Mine

A Litany of Loss

Lekarapa

1

My grandfather is dead
he was vomiting blood, my mother says
lungs contaminated by history
brimming full with mine dust.

He left, went,
he was always away
always leaving
a migrant laborer:
missed his first child's birth
his second, third, fourth, fifth, sixth.

When I last saw him he asked my mother
    "Who is this fine young man?"
My mother corrected him tenderly,
    She's your granddaughter, Papa.

He must have been washed with shame
triggered—haunted till his last days
by the recurrence of that question
each time he came home once a year
for Christmas.
Presented with a newborn, infant, toddler
    "And who is this fine little baby?"
She is your daughter, he is your son.

2

Rakgolo, did you have to kick your heart shut
when you met your stranger-children

these young babes with open mouths
and fledgling hearts?
Did you search their faces
looking for your eyes?
Did they fill a gulf
in your heart
broad with longing and love,
or did you feel like a stranger-father to them,
distance and time
informing your self-preservation?
Did your heart harden like scab on a wound?

How did you preserve the memories
of these people, this stranger-family of yours
when you were baking in earth's womb
feverish with yearning,
miscarrying all dreams of kin and family?

At what point, with no photograph,
no letter, no visitation
did your heart, your manhood
collapse into itself and give up dreams
of fatherhood, of community,
husband, uncle, brother, grandfather
as the months and years unravel
sludging forth with cruel hope?

At what point did you down tools
of digging and drilling and mining
futures where you are reunited
permanently with your blood?

Was it after the sixth union strike
when mine slopes collapsed

and buried your brothers alive?
Some under twenty years old
young bulls in their prime
locked in the pits of gold.
Was it then that you saw death
unmarked, unrecorded, and unceremonious
that you clearly understood
your insignificance?

When your demands for a pay raise
or better living conditions
or rights to have your wives visit the city
were laughable and met with scorn?

Was it the message from the Chamber of Mines
that made it blood-curdling clear:
    "Any miner who goes on strike shall be
    permanently banished to their homeland
    and their hut taxes quadrupled,
    failure to pay will be punishable by death."

3
Social death, communal death, familial death
ambiguous loss—
in which I miss you when you are here
in which I see you when you are not here
my mother's ambiguous loss of a father
Koko's ambiguous loss of a husband.
Rakgolo, your loss of centerpiece position
in your family and community
only to be a faceless pawn and cog in the wheel;
the loss of fatherhood when you had children
the loss of manhood when you were infantilized and called boy
the absence of your divine humanity in your ancestral land

to reside like a mole in middle earth
to love and to have, but to have to love only in abstraction
alive but only in sickness and never in health
in guaranteed poverty while unearthing wealth
till death do you impale; vomiting blood.

4
Rakgolo, did you dread coming home
to searching eyes and hearts
to strangers who were once kin
to impotent excitement and dreary celebrations?
Were your lungs already half-filled?
Could you breathe?

Did Christmas become a vicious test of faith?
Did the birth of Christ bring melancholy and shame?
His first breath mocking your shallow breathing
taunting your collapsing diaphragm?
Did you wish for death in the silent night?
To be lowered permanently in the tomb of the earth
tightly mummified to avoid any resurrection?

5
Where is the life I have come to live?
I live in deadly conditions of protracted absences
I am unavailable, a void in my family
ringing with loss, longing, loneliness, and shame
I am battered by the whip of history
there is no sanctuary
my mind is a terrifying adversary
there my family resides fatherless
there my livestock roams without a herder
there the rains fail to nourish the drought in my soul
I am parched, dried out, moisture leaking from my faith

I am a critical mess, broken and unmendable
I am a ghost of a father, a son, an apparition
living in pipedreams of my oppressors
I scare my own children
they wail when they see me
my neighbors offer halfhearted smiles
when stranger-kin December visitor comes
crack their jaded jaws making conversation

My wife mirrors my shame
she closes her heart against my name
I am the inglorious dead
I don't want or need or desire
my mother, her companion
preaches life:
"Leave a part of you here for us to live."
She promises death, she wants life
   my wife obliges
   her warmth nauseates me
   her softness fills me with dread
   I want to beat her skin
   till it ruptures my impenetrable heart
   drain the grief and sorrow in my soul
   my shame, my name, my pain
   leaking her forgotten dreams
   overripe and putrefying
   we swelter through pores, steaming abreast
   huffing—I cannot breathe—puffing mine dust
   feeling her pulsating under death,
   not breathing, hollowed by duty
   mocked by marital bliss-phemy
   hiding hurt and heart
   numbing memories of pleasures
   coveted and stolen elsewhere

In the pondering saltiness of the earth
sweaty lean bodies in the barracks
eighteen per cement dormitory
shuffling one on top of the other,
breathing raggedly through pores
excreting drunken fumes jammed
in the throat of my hand
driving desperately, pining
releasing pressured pleasure
under breath of shameful gasp
air rotten erotic like blood
thicker than oil and diamonds
thrashing our rawness, erecting
underground sky-rapers
simmering muscles
caked with mud of base desires
dominating logic of bodies fading into
another, gorging and pouring
loss and desire
heavy with lead
mocked by intimacies of elsewheres

6

Where is the marriage we came to live?
We slaughter a goat for life
for hearts afflicted with irreversible damage
we pour libations for divination
for poor health, for broken community.
We break.we mend.we scream.we shatter.you leave.

Moletelo

I

Black women in the coalface
of frontier capitalist wars:
Koko crippled becoming
a widowed newlywed
with a living husband
—married former wife—
a carnage of social anomaly
coming home to roost
with bright-eyed brides
tested by gold addiction
and Black abjection
haunted at night by monsters and shadows
who taunt their bedrooms,
intimate with Lonmin loss
wives without husbands
former mothers of sons

A vicious modernity
disfigures Black maternity
turns Black women's wombs
into factories producing blackness
wombs of profit and prophets
birth canal strengthening GDP
ushering their children
into nonstatus, nonbeing
Black women's birth canals
domestic middle passages[1]
forced to deliver sons
into the mine tomb of the state

a dehumanizing project
that traps mothers into
obligatory reproduction
to honor patriarchs
to honor capitalist duties
widows with living husbands
birthing sorrow and longing
youthful hearts gorged by grief
under patriarchal oath and code of silence:
we do not speak of our heartbreak
the depression, the inability to breathe
the lustful nights, the desire for flight
the foundering dreams of the city of lights
the unspoken rights to partake in the gold

We shall forget the newborn
the ones we buried and never talk about
the tongues we had to swallow in our mourning
trailed with bloodstains of memory
We shall master silence and forgetting

Grieving but not crying . . .

2

Rotating between pregnant and breastfeeding
Grieving a miscarriage and pregnant
Breastfeeding after a miscarriage
Grieving a stillbirth while pregnant
Bleeding a miscarriage while breastfeeding
Pregnant, grieving and miscarrying
Grieving infertility after still birth
Breeding, feeding, and bleeding
Breastfeeding a stillborn

while grieving a miscarriage
Grieving postnatal breeding

Ke motswetši ke imile ke a hloboga
Ke imile ke a hloboga ke motswetši
Ke motswadi wa go hloka sestswetši
Motswetši was go hloka lesea

Not waving but drowning

Grieving birthing boys that become profit
Hating love that grieves the heart
Closing heart against willful abduction
Grieving husbands who become profitable boys
Grieving stillbirth in the stillness of longing
Lusting grief in the breastfeeding of profitable boys
Miscarrying orgies of postnatal gross domestic loss

DO NOT CRY! O S'KA LLA!
Grieving but not crying...

3
In 1961 my grandmother went to the city
of lights with her husband
lodging hidden in the crevices of the cold compounds
the matriarchs orchestrated the visit
she wasn't ovulating when he was home
a mule with a practical agenda, two weeks tops
but the iciness of the city bonded their flesh longer
in the middle of the night a RAID
Knock knock BOOM crash
hide behind the curtain of history!
Under the blanket of white terror

Hey boy, what's this kaffir bitch doing here
She doesn't have a permit!
Sorry sorry sorry sorry sorry, baas
Hey bitch, this is not bloody Gazankulu
Don't look at me when I talk to you
Boy, does your wife know you play
with whores in this shack of yours?
Please please, sir, she is my wife
Our child just died and we are grieving
Hahahahaha listen to this kaffir acting white
mock tone my child just died . . .
I want her gone before the sun comes out!
and they were gone
leaving a flame of shame
licking clean all affection
bringing the weight of rage to crush
their disposable lives

DO NOT CRY! O S'KA LLA!
We do not speak about those things

4
The present is a tough terror to swallow
a contaminated place to breathe
artificial in-cemetery . . .
windows broken by inherited shame
Grief. Longing. Loss. Spiritual dis-ease.
the terror of leaving and never coming back
rageful outbursts of unprocessed grief
fermenting in the foaming mouth
swelling inflamed sprouting outgrowths
history is brewing in my uterus
fibroiding and braiding my past
with a present that triggers minefields

Miners Shot Down!! My mother's
neurosis ruptures her psychic spleen
a mental hiccup, reflex gag
mineral heartburn of a tumor
in the belly of her beauty
the mark of the beast
I am of her, of her embodied grief
body an inventory of leaving
Black rage in swallow. My skin
a pathology of violent encounters
an inhalation of fibric intimacies
a memorial to enforced labor

5

How do you raise daughters to be widows?
To be the most unmarried married women
to mother without fathers
to break flowers in their mouth
to live with aftertaste of extermination?
They must excel at swallowing grief
kneel at the altar of duty
martyr themselves in their father's honor
be eloquently unsung
be obedient to loss
—especially of self!—
too many grievances spoil the rot
a calculus of Black female death
There's.No.Space.For.Your.Tears.Here.

Your depression offends me
the weak die before they are born
and, girl, you are going to live
even if it kills you!
Do you know the troubles I've seen?

Do you not know what troubles
lie ahead for a Black woman like yourself?
I need to toughen you up!
I would have failed
if I didn't prepare you for the world
that's not set up for you and me
a system that makes cemeteries of us
that lowers coffins of our husbands
in us, in our bowels, in our throats
sons that don't make it back
husbands that husband and father
other families ko Maboneng
we've buried daughters like you
daughters like us, for they brought grief
won't even look at you!
Young bulls are prized: boys boys boys
we were born widows
into this condition that doesn't have a name
a mother without children
a neurosis of history

6

Sons and daughters were tortured in prison
chopped up and braaied
by cannibals of the state
brain-damaged by torture
then dragged behind a bakkie
disemboweled, decapitated, maimed
These.Bodies.Return.To.Mothers.And.Wives
unadorned by the national flag . . .
to bright-eyed daughters and sons
whose sparkling suns set before their prime
How do I receive their dismembered parts?
How do I re-member the dismembered?

We are born in a blanket,
come of age with a blanket
Then the blanket of our womanhood
The gift blanket of our marriage
Of our first child, second child
The blanket to mourn our miscarriage
Stillbirth, not breathing, under a blanket
The blanket you bring from Egoli
a declaration of our love
The blanket to mourn you when you
don't return, when you return dead
decapitated, maimed, disemboweled
The blanket of devastation
to hide my pain and tears
Incantatory sobs of a praying mantis
under a blanket, a kanga
A macabre honor code
of broken wishbones
from sacrificial cocks
crushed by silence
burying violence
like seeds
firing up future soils
here and
forever more

O S'KA LLA! DON'T CRY!

I cannot breathe

Makgolwa

I

A vicious and calamitous modernity
waging underground industrial wars[2]
producing a staggering 40 percent of the world's gold
and with it, a tenfold of generational casualties
In the frontier city of Egoli, Gauteng, Jozi Maboneng
a buzzing metropolis fueled by Black death
The Black migrant worker
forced into compliance, obedience—
feared and desired,
policed, marshalled, disciplined
hounded, chased, trapped, incarcerated;
broken into animal.

Police pester pedestrians for passes
Dompas dompas my life my wife
Hungry hand comes back with nothing
from the rear pocket
Where is your pass, boy?
Now I ride in the kwela-kwela
Heavy air massive with song and solidarity
Moments of clamoring clarity
    AMANDLA! AWETHU!
    MAYIBUYE! iAFRIKA
In jail we eat political education
wash it down with revolution
amid rats, cockroaches, and ticks

In the mines we get shorn like black sheep
The prisons shave us like disease-infested infidels

Our lungs are filled with silicosis in the mines
We are asphyxiated in the prisons
Lungs riddled with tuberculosis
We cannot breathe—drowning
in the blood of tortured comrades
who fell from the ninth floor
by slipping on a piece of soap while washing
by hanging on the ninth floor while slipping[3]
White lies infiltrating radioactive waves
of international press
THE NATIVES ARE RESTLESS
says one headline, while prisoners'
heads are in the firing line
My grandfather toeing the line
of secretly throwing Black fist in the air
while playing docile drilling the gold standard
of white monopoly

2

America,
    America,
            arbiter of morality
enemy of dirty communists
assisting apartheid apprehend and assassinate
Black antiracist activists through severe surveillance
and perverse alliances to subdue revolution
    Jim Crow and apartheid sitting in a tree
    K-I-L-L-I-N-G
    Apartheid and Thatcher sitting in a tree
    K-I-S-S-I-N-G
    French-kissing federal intelligence
building iron curtains with our gold
intercepting and infiltrating insurrections
chasing imagined red peril and rooi gevaars

"We will protect our right to pillage Africa
for natural resources by any means necessary
trample them with the might of our first world
We are America!
These kaffirs and niggers don't know the real
cost of the civilization they enjoy
We will crush any savage and barbarian
who wants to stop progress
You can count on us, Verwoerd
We locked away that terrorist Sobukwe
We provided intel for Liliesleaf Farm raid
where those bloody savages and nigger lovers
thought they could bring the Algerian revolution
to South Africa. They will rot in jail, yes sir!"

Abelungu ngoddam
Abelungu ngoddam
Basibiza abo-Jim
Mississippi Goddam!
Mississippi Goddam!
Basibiza abo-Jim

3
He came as one, my grandfather
but stood with millions
from rural homelands
Tanzania, Namibia, Zambia, Rhodesia,
Nyasaland, Swaziland, Basutoland
Those deemed raw savages, primitive natives
swallowed by the train, stimela sa malahla
mixed with cattle and coal on freight trains
bringing with them languages and praise poets
spiritual forms, traditional practices
cultural artefacts and choreographies

they were disgorged in the pits of gold
Time ticking for turnaround track

Train.Tirelessly.Returning.To.Fetch.More

On a railroad made of human bones
at the bottom of the Atlantic
conjoining with human teeth
below the cape of storms
masters get shipwrecked
slaves get bodywrecked
vision calcified, caked
with cavities of coral reef
on the way to gold reef
City of Atlantis
with residents from Indonesia, India, Malaysia
Mauritius, Madagascar, Mozambique
the ones who were enslaved in the Cape.

    After abolishment of slavery
    when diamonds were discovered in Kimberley
    emancipated slaves were arrested en masse
    put in prisons where they were trapped once more
    and posted to go work in those mines—
    De Beers operated early prisons and mining compounds
    paid the state for use of their prisoners
    to meet their demand for cheap labor.[4]
    In the same way mining compounds
    in Johannesburg were built by the Oppenheimers
    the state accepted a loan of six million
    from Robert Oppenheimer to build
    Soweto's infamous matchbox houses
    which were reservoirs for labor
    mechanizing and merchandizing the Black body.

Profitable men in chains
prisons bolstering GDP
hunting and taming boys
controlling their movements
burying them alive—
legacies of slavery
now archived in the muscles of Black men.

The Cape cohort of mining labor
brought their goema
their languages and movements
their foods and spices and spiritual expressions.
They who sailed in the womb of the ship
those whose lungs are filled with saltwater
of the Atlantic and Indian, casualties of the middle passage
residing in the womb-tomb of the ocean, unable to breathe
from the hold of the ship to holding cells,
to mine hostels, the final grave
of mice and men
of underground people, moles, and mules
never to see the sun again
pawns in our breathless and breath-taking civilization
water-logged, dust-clogged lungs
in the furnace, caked into bricks
to lay foundations for erecting sky-raping edifices
palpitating and perspiring through wall streets
into conglomerates of free market global franchises
that capitalize on our disenfranchisement.

Abelungu ngoddam
Abelungu ngoddam
Basibiza abo-Jim
Mississippi Goddam!
Mississippi Goddam!
Basibiza abo-Jim

4

He came as one, my grandfather
but stood as millions
a brilliant battalion
that refused death in life
names that in dying make life surer than death.

    They left us a treasure trove,
    animating the supremacy of spirit.
    They are our mythologies, our inheritance
    a tapestry of Fanagalo cultures.
    They forged lives from their own ashes
    made languages in caverns of their mouths
    speaking in tongues wrapped around waves of the Atlantic
    saliva trailing tracks of traversed bantu terrains
    exploding tsotsitaal, patois, creole, into our future
    ocean and land in a liberatory dance
    kaapse klopse and pantsulas in a "kwaito klopse"[5]
    tantalizing creators of cosmopolitan identities
    the hip kings, tsotsis, city slickers, abokleva
    moegoes, plaasjapies, baries, moemish
    maskandi, penny-whistlers, marabi, jazz, kwela
    creating in captivity against the limits of the spirit
    richer than any gold
    refusing death, resisting the social order
    undermining it through movement.
"Force. Creative power.
The walk of Sophiatown tsotsi or
a Harlem brother on Lenox Avenue.
Field hollers. The blues. Work songs.
A John Coltrane riff.
Marvin Gaye or mbaqanga.
Anguished happiness.

Creative power, released,
moving like a dancer's muscle,.
hearing the strained laughter of distant hearts,
stomping the ear of the world,
asserting the supremacy of spirit."[6]

Black Rage in Swallow

I

Cross-dressed to board the train
on which only virile men are allowed
swallowed by white desire for boys, boys, boys
for jims and johns,
under the solemn gaze of conductor
sits in suits and pants
the wayward Black women
who refuse the destiny of their lives.
Like flight from the plantation,
the escape from slavery,
the migration from the South,
the rush into the city,
Black women fled the countryside
where they were fated to
continue rural production
their wombs rendered
factories of Black labor
reproducing blackness and abjection.
They refused their roles
carved from bone the choice to resist.
Likers of things, wayward and extra
they dared to imagine
the city of lights
strolls down Sophiatown streets,
choreography was their art,
a practice of moving even
when there's nowhere to go,
no place left to run.
    The swaying of hips on stages of song.

Swingsters, merrymakers, skylarks, diponono
arranging their bodies to elude capture,
efforts that make the uninhabitable livable,
to escape confinement of four cornered worlds,
and tight, airless matchbox houses.
"Tumult, upheaval, flight—
it was the articulation of living force,
it was the way to insist
I am unavailable for servitude. I refuse it."[7]

In the velvet bedroom suite
of her matchbox palace
forged out of cunning
and inherited streetsmarts
Dineo holds a lingering moment
of heat with Patience—
the most unmarried
wife of a gold reef miner
out of sight and plight
in the stealth of sweetness
a ferocious pang of longing
sultry embrace of buried desire
excavated under tongue
searches strange lands
inside wombs and canals
the deep exhale of earth's belly
rising and falling, secreting
convulsions that enrobe Black joy
in a blanket of song
midnight hour dark nurse
tending the archive
of loss in her heart
a crescendo of fitful
coming and going

to virgin territories of screams
primal pressure released
into caverns of history.

2

Khawuleza, Mama
Homeplaces as hotbeds of resistance:
children growing up with their grandmothers,
mothers and aunts witnessing
enterprising businesses from their homes
brewing and selling alcohol
baking scones, making magwinya
selling atchaar and cold drinks.
    Khawuleza, Mama,
    "Khawuleza" is a South African song—
    it comes from the townships,
    reservations, locations near Johannesburg.
    The children shout from the streets
    as they see police cars coming
    to raid their homes.
    They say, Khawuleza, Mama!
    which simply means,
    "Hurry up, Mama, and hide—
    Please don't let them catch you."[8]
Sending signals and whistles to womenfolk
to warn them of approaching police.
Embodying political currency
articulating resistance as everyday practice
harmonizing the community
with its call to revolt:
Khawuleza, Shosholoza
Black lives on the move
Black bodies in resonance.
Children socialized within refusal

inheriting collective suspicion of police
strengthening communal bonds,
and trust in urban Black communities.

Mam' Dorcas queen pin of the reef
owner of herself and many-a-man
curtailing many-a-legislation
skirting fictions of the state
shifting means of production
to her backyard, and turning shack
into palace of dreams
where revolutions are made
a veritable compound of stars
where hip identities are lived
Ma-authi in brentwood and dopsie
relishing dops of Mellowood
Charlie Mingus serenading the day
Kippie Moeketsi flowering nightfall
comrade poets reading banned literature
or smuggling records, paintings, and letters,
through Aus Dorcas's Swaziland connects
tsotsis brandishing knife skills of musketeers
putting holes in miner's weekly pay
gashing flesh with a gambling impulse.

3
Bevies of unbridled beauty
loud and intentional
about their Blackness
adorn the latest fashion
embellished in red Cutex
and leather figure belts
don Black Power berets
a cacophony of cackles

and reckless abandon
young lions crouching against
feral surveillance
Sheila's Day an assertion
of full humanity
turning body of labor
into body of leisure
claiming urban identities
in night classes
hiding political training
behind sewing and knitting
fashioning soft power
behind the eye of the hurricane:
Yes, revolutionary needlework!

4
Aus Matshidiso
called Mary by her medem
who loves dogs and tolerates Africans
Her home an embattled zone
of domestic surveillance
Dutiful discipline a daily routine
social warfare on Black female body
Hateful mine bosses give white wives
rights to prowl auction blocks
and hire house slaves whom they rename
Matshidiso now "girl," teagirl, maidgirl
Faithful white women embrace
white power and white wealth
wear sleeves of gold, and cloak
white terror, kleptocracy, cocky pride
enjoy spoils of their men's exploits.
     Their husbands only see Black women
          during enactments of male power

Defile us in front of their wives
in the refuge of their castles
cut our face with bones
of their scorned ribcage
suckle their spawn adam
on the bleak bounty of our body
wet nurse against the aesthetic
of their breast, to be
perked and firmer
in richness and in health
for husband's tenderness
after he's drained his violence in us.
A lapse in judgement
of momentary fall from grace
tempted by the devil
with an insatiable appetite.
White women call us whores
Black men call us whores
see us as sites of conquest
that mock their shame
smack us in the face
for getting hit by racing
horse carts of their master's
virile mshini weaponized—
We, receipts of deceit in
the servants' quarter
where adam you suckled
comes of age in threadbare linens
a rites of baas passage
historical master copy
of the fathers' original sin
braiding the raiding
of my grandmother's body
with the fibroid of my daughter.

5

Comrade Khwezi
sobered by precarity of Blackness
of living in the violence
of a waiting room
joined the ranks of forces
jumped barbed wire fences
into heart of darkness
searching for light of liberation
through comrade crocodile jaws
craving her tender flesh
fresh with raw desire.
Recalling survival tips
she stabs him in the eye
but being in a movement
where one-eyed comrades
are hailed as heroes
in parades of strength
and uniformed ceremonies
of primordial social hierarchies
predatory sizing of the wilderness
Blood of life and death embroiling
on the thrashing floor of battlefield
biting and gasping trusted cadre
heating his shrill weapon
in the natural oven of the savannah
fighting for man's freedom
and nationalization of the mine
mine mine mine
ownership paradigm exported
from the auction block
to unequal power relations
of court rulings

using laws
our rapists wrote
to put our rapists
on trial!
Amandla, ngawethu madoda

6

We inherit wounds of broken men
the abandonment of our grandmothers
our mother's grief, longing—
their ambiguous loss
Don't tell me to smile
I am afflicted by my mother's rage
I inherit unprocessed grief
sitting in my womb as tumors
maligning reproductive cancers
Our collective inheritance
is gorged bodies
And terror in the streets—
Maimed lovers father our children
rape us in our marital beds
disembowel lesbian lovers
torture transbodies
decapitate us for gold
mutilate our tongues
bury us alive
impaled, vomiting blood . . .

Grieving but not crying
O S'KA LLA!

Ancestral Suite

I

My grandfather's life was difficult,
my mother says. His life after retirement
was a ground zero of disgrace.
He came home without a cent
throughout his working life.
He had to choose: honor in life or in death.
The inhuman barracks provided by the mines
were filthy, disease-riddled pigsties.
A man who comes from a pride of women
who holds high hygiene and home keep
to take abode with lice, flies, and mice
in a hovel short on lighting or ventilation
was to give into nonhuman status
was to accept the final bludgeoning.
Rakgolo had to find alternative lodging
which came with a price in the city of gold
and a heavier price in unmaking his family—
He rented a room in the township
and, coming from a place of communal love
found living alone to double his exile.
On a lonesome night at Mme Dorcas's den
of city pleasures, brandy, and politiki
a practical logical love blossomed
from the darkness of secrecy
to the light of coveted wonderment
of a heart long shut to affection.
Distance offered an illusion of newness
of secret family known but never talked of
in new language, new clothes, new moral code

modern house, modern wife, new children
a double-story constructed on country and city
stacking two worlds scaffolded by your heart.

Rakgolo, did you name your city children
after family members, as custom dictates?
Do we share names with your stranger-family?
Were you present at their births?
Are they reciting your lineage
with a double-forked tongue?
Did that soothe your yearning and pining?
Did your heart flower or
become a weeping willow
of staggering guilt and regret?
Where is this family of ours,
our kin of the golden city?
Do they suppress bile
of disappointment and abandonment,
and unanswered questions?
Do they suffer afflictions
of their history written
with blood of missing kin?
What are their names?
Khumbul'ekhaya rakgolo . . .
The wreathing and delirium
on your deathbed. Was it
a haunting of two worlds
both asphyxiated
by the chokehold of history?

2

He never got a retirement fund, of course
There are bodies of labor and bodies of leisure
To be sure, labor is Black, leisure is white

Only bodies of leisure get retirement funds
because they occupy the category of human
where family time, holidays, and connection are vital
Bodies of leisure control the time, energy, and fate
of labor. Miners were not allowed watches;
their time, days, and months were kept for them.
Rakgolo would be dismissed and reappointed
for his retirement package to be affected—
His dompas stamped with "citizen non grata"
banished to the god-forsaken homeland
to be attacked with missiles of mockery
Mahlalela, Mahlalela—a man who sits all day
watching other men work for their families!
To avoid disgrace, you go back
burrow in the pipes away from the police
until you find another mill to grind you
subjected to medical tests
scrutinizing the health of your lungs;
such is the abomination
and irony of civilization

3
At the height of slavery in America
slave labor generated more profit
than railways and factories combined
Enslaved workforce was where
the country's wealth resided
South African capitalism
did one up on American slavery
Here slavery, factory, and railway
conjugated in a threesome
of unholy trinity
to power global capitalism,
to build and sustain NATO world power

long after slavery had been abolished
in most of the world

On the WitwatersRAND
where the RAND was coined
and minted by horsemen
on broken bones of bereft brothers
building a globally competitive rand
they could never pocket—
like "In God We Trust" on the dollar
The gods trusted by the masters
in Deep South of Africa and America
were our gods—badimo—our grandfathers
fed to insatiably ravenous Christian overseers . . .
In a cunning distortion of history
the original sin was invented
to deflect from the paramount sin
of colonial expansion and white terrorism
in which our fathers, sons, and husbands
connived with the serpent and fell from grace
Born of sin and eternally damned
to be exploited and pillaged
like the nature which tempted them

Sons of Ham
condemned to slavery
where race was made
where rape was profit
we were commodity.
We become the coal we mine
the cotton we pick
the sugarcane we reap
the tobacco we cultivate
the grapes we harvest

Swallowing centuries of horror
the coal became our lungs
the cotton became our noose
the sugarcane our diabetes
the grapes our alcoholism
the gold our centuries-old debt
the tobacco our enduring inability to breathe
a bronchital history that afflicts Black life
lungs filled with silicosis, asbestosis, tuberculosis
We reap what is sown by superhuman greed
The dop system reaped in the plantations of the Cape
makes us today's leaders in alcohol consumption
"Our hands wove the patterns of the vineyards
Our feet pressed the grapes
And we were paid with wine
We carry fetal alcohol syndrome
children on our backs"[9]
Breathtaking statistics of femicide and rape
History's drunken violence courses through our veins
We are the sugar at the bottom of the English teacup[10]
White gold, the British call Sugar
Enslaved, killed, maimed, and raped for it,
disemboweled, decapitated our being for it

4
In Brazil gold miners are made to
work naked to avoid theft
The bitter irony of colonial thieves
as courts of law, truth, and justice
A striptease of a men-turned-boys.

　　Rakgolo subjected to the same humiliation
　　morning routines of cowboys and natives
　　of hide and seek for nuggets of gold

searched and destroyed in nether regions
of Ernest Cole's surviving record.
Made to bend over
gloved hands thrust within
made to search each other
part of guards' locker-room boyish fun
of taming the haughty native
that continued to stand tall beyond his shame
We will put him in line
through a public "baton body search"
a brutality of sodomic butchery
to teach others a lesson against pride
We will whip your ass
cut your fingers, toes, and hands
like the Belgians in the Congo
We will make you strip, search,
and whip other miners . . .
You are nothing to us!

We reap the humiliation of poverty sown
in the upward mobility of our gold and diamonds,
sold back to us as American Swiss
grinning in eternal gratitude
for scant AngloGold scholarships.
Foreign investors funding Afrophobic violence
through a murderous culture of scarcity
While global economy is bankrolled
by Black maternity, white theft—
We slobber in indignity of betrayal
quaffing fast food with our amnesia
watching our death toll with resigned indignance

5

Kill them, use concomitant force,
was the instruction
from Cyril killer
A thuma bona to
kill—a mambush
    sing I don't wanna be there
    when the police are mowing them down
    I just wanna issue the command
    Thina saaa—thuma yena, thuma yena.
Wrestling with the wrangling
arm of time around our necks
The perversity of anti-Black
racism by Black leaders
Stlamatlama
Sa apartheid reloading

The meek shall inherit violence
When orphaned children
witness the birth of a nation
they want to avenge their fathers
When uncles subdue their violence,
their alienation and abandonment
they empty their rage in their nieces

Lefa la Ntate

I

Lefa la ntate
Ke mahloko le maswabi
Le boitsholo ba go fenywa
Ba go hlabisa dihlong
Ba go hloka mantswe
Ba go omisa leleme

Ba mo tseetse botho
A sa phela
Ba mo tseela
Polelo a sa nale molomo
Ba mo tseela lentswe
A sa nale leleme

Motho ke sera
Seo fela se rego
Ge se rakeletswe
Se se na leleme
Se lahle botho
Se hlabane ka marumo[11]

Our inheritance
is deep disgrace, shame
silence and defeat
that dries our mouths
and leaves deserts
in our souls

My grandfather's humanity
was taken while he was alive
his language broken in his mouth
his tongue severed and buried

A human being
is a beast that when cornered
and its tongue taken
throws away his humanity
and fights ferociously with weapons

2

When state colludes with capital
when the capital you built
with your lungs, humanity, and dignity
renders you a wasted life
a surplus population to purge
you fight your animal
Your animal fights you
when the blood of revolution
fought in the underground of exile
does not converge with your own
flowing in the underground of the mines
You become your animal
when heroes of the day
are only those who wielded guns
when you were oiling
the machine with your sweat
You become animal
when Black skin takes over
white capital
when Black skin apes

white violence
You kill your heart
and attack to survive
You survive, never live

3
A ring of fire
bonds Black women
to dutiful fits of historical rage
unprocessed grief
archived in the muscle of Black men,
outlet for centuries of exploitation
subjection, and breaking of Black power,
internalized, brewed, now fermenting
toxic malignant masculinities
infecting Black women
Controlling their movements
Disciplining and punishing them
Burying them alive
centenaries of vengeful agony
trapped in double stories
of mineshaft homes
with evil leers of overseers
slopes kept from crashing on our backs
toiling in search of the shiny appearance
digging deep enough to bury our dreams
the forbidden deadly sin of pride
there can be only one bull in the kraal
suffocating, pleasure-faking under the bull
clawing for promises of our covenant
of church hymns, amens, and hymens
Breaking back so he can rise
Breaking hymen for his honor
Breaking mouth for his status

Breaking my name.so.he.can.possess.me
Breaking, breaking, breaking
    Break your body for my lineage
    Break your body for my children
    Breastfeed my children
    Don't breastfeed in public
    Fix your saggy breasts
    to breastfeed me
    Climb ladders of success
    But don't pass me
    Make money but give it to me
    Doctor at work, wife at home
    CEO in the office, slave in my kitchen
    Make dombolo, make lasagna
    Don't wear waist beads
    unless on top of me
    Don't talk back to me
    Don't ask me questions
    Don't take birth control
    Don't be pregnant again
    Don't have an abortion
    Why are you pregnant again?
    Be a mother and a virgin
    Be a whore in my bed
    Be conservative and respectable
    Be adventurous. Kiss a girl
    Only for my pleasure
Don't.be.a.whore.outside.my.house!
Restore your birth canal,
Be a virgin, be a mother
Bleach your vagina and your face
I don't like makeup
I like tall dark dandies
Be a yellow-bone Lupita

I hate to love you
I hate to hate you
I love to hate you
I hate hating me
I hate your heart
I hurt my heart
I heart my hate
I hunger to howl
H.E.L.P
I hurt, I hurt, I hurt

4

Lefa la ntate
Ke mahloko le maswabi
Le boitsholo ba go fenywa
Ba go hlabisa dihlong.

Leaving,
always going—
knowing going
more than staying
intimate with loss
and abandonment
sons' mouths parched
from asking about fathers
daughters hollowed
by yearning validation
bone-deep cuts of history
revealing marrow encoding
DNA of absence and death
mourning in the morning
bellicose homes of rupture
throwing up bulimic futures
of entrapment and suffocation

codes of secrecy and silence
pushing down the pain
with Big Mac of Cyril
and ribs of blessers
invading our privates
clogging arteries to numb
the voices of ancestors
demanding reckoning
cleansing and restoring
cracking our cranium
with cocaine for the pain
of not knowing
where our dead are buried
not knowing the song
of our lineage
not knowing our sthakazelo
not knowing where
our fathers are
not knowing who we are
not waving but drowning
not breathing but living
not living but surviving
not knowing the violence
of our past
repeated in the safety
of our homes

5
I hit a fit of hell
Unhome my
house of hunger
Hollowed by
heinous history
Unhinged,

I hunt your hurt
And hurt your heart
Turn the hate
On hanging
my hollow home
in cold blood
The horror!
I hit my heart
Habitually hurt
my hate
of hardship
it's hard—
I hate my hurt
I hurt, it hurts
It's hard, it hurts . . .

6

But did we die?
Yes, we did die
found salvation from whoredom
and lascivious eyes of the master
salivating over harems on plantations
and servants' quarters.
Black bodies on strike
self-immolate for transcendence.
Out of the ruins and smolder
of remarkable destruction,
in the thick silence
of starry darkness,
the blackness of creation,
a vision and a voice:
"Do not be afraid
You have found
favor and redemption:

Unto you daughters
shall be born
with medicine
for the lineage
in the bones of
their tongues."

Yes, we did die,
in the blackness
of destruction and creation.
We part our hips
like the sea
and birth ourselves,
use our mothers' names
to sing our resurrection,
weave our purpose with gifts
from three wise womxn
who imprinted scriptures
forged out of stardust
and spectacular smithereens
of our former selves
into quilts of our hearts.
Moonlight illuminates
our new name: the dying wish
of burning mouths
blazing in our bones
blossoming with revelations
of our spirit supreme.

Unburied

A moment of silence
to listen to the good book
(not written in your language):
gather your first born sons
and all adult males
as offerings of your race
to the shrine of modernity

Close your eyes
and observe a moment
of deep listening—
the drilling
in the heart of
ancestral man
thundering terror
gorging his underworld
to unearth spirit—
the diamond in the
coalface of history

Open your inner eye
and feel the pulse
of preternatural fear—
letswalo, ivalo—
undulating audacity
to corner and accost
those at rest
stabbed awake by
grand theft of
jewels in the earth

Close your eyes
and witness in the stillness
the hollowing of the stolen,
our gutting and scraping
by a benevolent mission
extracting our spirits
directly out of our bodies
powered by
the sweat of our brow.
The fall from pastoral heaven
into the golden gates of
mercantile hell.
Hollowed be our names

Open the bone of your heart
and feel the smells,
the screams of fire flame
licking melanated flesh
spontaneous combustion of
sulfuric biosphere
gaseous breath ignited
by power failures of body count!
A blackout

Close your eyes and see
the scattered bones:
Collaterals
of colonial conquest
unburied
Excavated without libation
The living dead
whisper thunderous command
ceremony! ceremony!
Where is the ritual
the song and prayer?
Here, now. Hear us
Here, hear, here, hear

Close your eyes and hear
the wail of grandmother
for the seed in the earth
that rots in the violence
of the underworld
shooting from earth
without sprouts to nourish
deserted hearts
mouthing supplications
to petition presence
and grace from the grave

Mother is spirit
father is body
son is brain drain
in the parched
threefold cord of
our unburied present

Here lies your monuments
your battle warriors
your venerated mothers
godheads of ancient altars
figurines of your memory
Here lies ceremonial herbs
shattered gourds and clay pots
abandoned in unburied graves
Here. Hear the song of your blood[12]

There are gods here—
shrines of your sacrifices
horns of your medicines
cords of your births
bones of your death
cowhides of your royals
breath of ancestral prayers:
songs of your rebirth

Sacraments of Unburying
  1. Light a fire (candles)
  2. Offer sacrifice (blood, salt)
  3. Sing their names (invocation)
  4. Burn sage (smoke, incense)
  5. Pour libation (water, mqombothi)
  6. Make offerings (snuff, sweets)
  7. Speak to bones (appease, listen)
  8. Unearth bones (Makhosi!)
  9. Sing their names (supplicate)
  10. Rebury the bones (sing "Thina Sizwe")

Attune yourself to the scream
of night terrors compounded
by wraths of unburied wreathes
the swallowed bellow of
sacramental bulls leading
bleeding souls through
the golden capital
drumming footsteps
the sole of the new master's boot

We gravitate toward soil
sink our fingers deep
excavate bone and living flesh
listen to the ground
for our fathers, brothers
husbands and sons
in the heart of dust
damp, and darkness
a directive for Black
pregnant women to eat soil
and keep sons safely buried
in their wombs
away from the tombs of the mines
Maternal instinct to protect
mutilation of Black labor

PART 2

State of Mine

Deeds

Mines are the key site
to study the unholy trinity
and afterlives
of Dutch slavery,
British colonialism,
and apartheid
in South Africa

History in my body,
a history of personalities
and lords of war
dominant in muscle memory.
History that turns the tide
of centuries-old violence
against us, the unspoken and unsung.
I write this history
residing in my body.
It resounds yours too.
In speaking of widows and wives of history,
we speak to ourselves.
When it dies a violent death,
as it often does, history returns
to wives and grandmothers.
And children too,
protected by the water of their mothers' bodies.
We are those children,
and, like water, we remember.
History's tide swells within us in full moon,
during the constant endings and beginnings
of our bodies remaking themselves.
With blood.
Every month.
Blood that separates us
from our fathers and brothers
in the mosque.
We sing its name:
our foremothers' refrain.[1]

When men exchanged power
from colonialism to apartheid
to CODESA rainbow.
The violence used to sustain
those oppressive white regimes
was imported to the era
of our governance.
The male repressed violence
that failed to find its logical conclusion
through armed confrontation
of the white other
exploded onto the female
and queer body.

Dana[2] says we must get out of the ghetto
let's backtrack and evacuate the mines
our state of minds are state of mines
Black bodies in colonial state capture
reproducing brokenness and death
refracting rainbows on our psyches

Evacuating mines
that produce the Black condition
is unlearning asphyxiation
learning how to breathe,
refusing death in life
minute-by-minute
A matter of unmaking
unpatterning and rewiring
our minds and spirits
A deliberate and intentional
radical persistent choice
to resist the toxicity
of our inherited disorder

Choosing the comfort zone
is electing to breathe mine dust
when there is oxygen,
to breathe underwater[3]
when there is land[4]
It is sensing freedom
but opting for captivity

The collusion of
postapartheid state
and capital
corrodes the soul
of the natives,
dis-indigenizes their bodies,
reproduces nervous condition,
cognitive dissonance,
extending the hold of the mine
to the hold of ghettoes
corporate office blocks
prisons of free market
that arrest our development
in mines of Black captivity

Living in a mine state
is running a race
lugging an
elephantine leg

giving birth in anti-Black
antinatal care[5]
raising children
in capital punishment state
disciplining their bodies
privatizing their minds
sacrificing their tongues
at the altar of plantations,
ripe for the picking

The underground
is our aesthetic
our myth
our language
our holey grail

The mine
plantation
ocean floor
prison

is the subaltern
in submarine
and subterrain

where we stand our ground

a familiar territory
of familial terror
where we broke
and resurrected

Coral reef to gold reef
the sound and chorus
of the Black subaltern
in the submarine
and subterranean
defiled and refined
by the furnace
of earth's urn
meets death
in flights of song:
The choral wreath
resounding gumboot
from the gutter
to the gut
of our ear[6]

Afrophobic violence
is the rupture of centuries-old
repressed violence
within miners
against white overlords,
boiling in the underground
exploding on the surface
of landless democracy
and Black capitalism,
raging against wretchedness
of the continent

A constitutional court ruling
declares it illegal to spank children at home
Incensed parents shoot tempers
and ruffle feathers
Fighting for rights
to flog their children,
to whip them like they were
whipped
during wartime

"Black women likely to suffer
from severe uterine fibroids"
Medical reasons unknown!
Speculation cites
diet, weight, alcohol
Even hair relaxers and shampoo

Colonial sexual warfare
is not suspected
Systemic rape
and terror of invasion
are not cited

High infant mortality rate,
swallowing and entombing
grief, loss, and mourning,
burying children and husbands
in cemeteries of our bodies
don't make the list

White boot to pregnant stomach
gynecological experiments
historical insemination
forced sterilization
high maternal death risk
natal and postnatal neglect
are not culprits

Our bodies are voids
in which history
casts its shameful acts
Our bodies are vaults
storing trauma that still breathes.
In.our.wombs

At no point in his-
story has white
woman breast-
fed gaping Black
babe mouth
involuntarily

Today's trash
is put out
by white desire
after it
broke in

we become cleaners

#menaretrash?

These two truths hold:
we defied death
with indomitable spirits
we were also scathed,
our memory banks
invaded and hacked

They call it the spiritual turn
because they arrive now.
We were always here

They call it a historic turn
because history
to them is political.
For us
it is self-regard
'cause history
lives in our bodies

When they mined our souls
they didn't talk conservation

ss Mendi
John Voster Square
Marikana
these.bodies.return.to.mothers.and.wives.
without medals.
without national flags.
if they return at all

"Broken heart"
still not
formalized as
"cause of death"

We inherited
two worlds,
both broken.
In one we are mocked
in the other
we mock ourselves

Calling our knowledge "indigenous"
locks it in prehistory,
to the dark before their light;
ties it to land stolen,
mystifies it and makes it foreign
new and western
when it is repackaged
and sold back to us

Gold and diamond mining
is the white pot
at the beginning
of the rainbow
nation

NOTES

PART 1. MINE

1. Adaptation of Christina Sharpe's *In the Wake: On Blackness and Being.*
2. This is Charles van Onselen's formulation in his brilliant *The Night Trains.*
3. Inspired by Chris van Wyk's poem "In Detention."
4. From Gabeba Baderoon's illuminating piece "The Creation of Black Criminality in South Africa."
5. A formulation by Benjamin Jephta in his lecture "Born Colored: Not 'Born Free.'"
6. From Keorapetse Kgositsile's "A Poet's Credo," published in the *Negro Digest,* July 1968.
7. Cited from the exquisite book *Wayward Lives, Beautiful Experiments* by Saidiya Hartman.
8. Miriam Makeba's song "Khawuleza."
9. From Diana Ferrus's poem "My Name Is February."
10. This line is from Stuart Hall's essay "Old and New Ethnicities," 1991.
11. A remix of O. K. Matsepe as cited by Phaswane Mpe in his *Welcome to Our Hillbrow.*
12. This stanza is after Derek Walcott's "The Sea Is History."

PART 2. STATE OF MINE

1. This stanza is after Ama Codjoe's "Burying Seeds."
2. Referring to Simphiwe Dana's song "Sizophum'elokishini" from her 2006 album, *The One Love Movement on Bantu Biko Street.*

3. In conversation with the line "breathe, you are not drowning" by Sizakele Phohleli.
4. You can't fight for land when you can't breathe.
5. Black women are six times more likely to die from complications surrounding pregnancy, during or after delivery, than white women.
6. This stanza is after Ishion Hutchinson's "The Wanderer."

IN THE AFRICAN POETRY BOOK SERIES

Exodus
'Gbenga Adeoba
Foreword by Kwame Dawes

After the Ceremonies:
New and Selected Poems
Ama Ata Aidoo
Edited and with a foreword
by Helen Yitah

The Promise of Hope: New and
Selected Poems, 1964–2013
Kofi Awoonor
Edited and with an introduction
by Kofi Anyidoho

Modern Sudanese Poetry:
An Anthology
Translated and edited
by Adil Babikir
Foreword by Matthew Shenoda

The Future Has an Appointment
with the Dawn
Tanella Boni
Translated by Todd Fredson
Introduction by Honorée
Fanonne Jeffers

There Where It's So Bright in Me
Tanella Boni
Translated by Todd Fredson
Foreword by Chris Abani

The Careless Seamstress
Tjawangwa Dema
Foreword by Kwame Dawes

Your Crib, My Qibla
Saddiq Dzukogi

The January Children
Safia Elhillo
Foreword by Kwame Dawes

Madman at Kilifi
Clifton Gachagua
Foreword by Kwame Dawes

Think of Lampedusa
Josué Guébo
Translated by Todd Fredson
Introduction by John Keene

In the Net
Hawad
Translated from the French
by Christopher Wise
Translated from Tuareg
(Tamajaght) into French by the
poet and Hélène Claudot-Hawad
Foreword by Hélène
Claudot-Hawad

Beating the Graves
Tsitsi Ella Jaji

Keorapetse Kgositsile:
Collected Poems, 1969–2018
Keorapetse Kgositsile
Edited and with an introduction
by Phillippa Yaa de Villiers
and Uhuru Portia Phalafala

'mamaseko
Thabile Makue

Stray
Bernard Farai Matambo
Foreword by Kwame Dawes

The Rinehart Frames
Cheswayo Mphanza
Foreword by Kwame Dawes

Gabriel Okara: Collected Poems
Gabriel Okara
Edited and with an introduction
by Brenda Marie Osbey

Sacrament of Bodies
Romeo Oriogun

The Kitchen-Dweller's Testimony
Ladan Osman
Foreword by Kwame Dawes

Mine Mine Mine
Uhuru Portia Phalafala

Mummy Eaters
Sherry Shenoda
Foreword by Kwame Dawes

Fuchsia
Mahtem Shiferraw

Your Body Is War
Mahtem Shiferraw
Foreword by Kwame Dawes

In a Language That You Know
Len Verwey

Logotherapy
Mukoma Wa Ngugi

Breaking the Silence: Anthology
of Liberian Poetry
Edited by Patricia Jabbeh Wesley

When the Wanderers Come Home
Patricia Jabbeh Wesley

Seven New Generation African
Poets: A Chapbook Box Set
Edited by Kwame Dawes
and Chris Abani
(Slapering Hol)

Eight New-Generation African
Poets: A Chapbook Box Set
Edited by Kwame Dawes
and Chris Abani
(Akashic Books)

New-Generation African Poets:
A Chapbook Box Set (Tatu)
Edited by Kwame Dawes
and Chris Abani
(Akashic Books)

New-Generation African Poets:
A Chapbook Box Set (Sita)
Edited by Kwame Dawes
and Chris Abani
(Akashic Books)

New-Generation African Poets:
A Chapbook Box Set (Nne)
Edited by Kwame Dawes
and Chris Abani
(Akashic Books)

New-Generation African Poets:
A Chapbook Box Set (Saba)
Edited by Kwame Dawes
and Chris Abani
(Akashic Books)

New-Generation African Poets:
A Chapbook Box Set (Tano)
Edited by Kwame Dawes
and Chris Abani
(Akashic Books)

New-Generation African Poets:
A Chapbook Box Set (Nane)
Edited by Kwame Dawes
and Chris Abani
(Akashic Books)

To order or obtain more information on these or other University of
Nebraska Press titles, visit nebraskapress.unl.edu. For more information
about the African Poetry Book Series, visit africanpoetrybf.unl.edu.

CPSIA information can be obtained
at www.ICGtesting.com
Printed in the USA
LVHW100345260123
737905LV00002B/243

9 781496 235152